The popular TV series makes its DVD debut!
SHONEN JUMP'S
NARUTO™
Meet Naruto Uzumaki: A ninja-in-training whose talent is overshadowed by his antics. But he has a hidden talent that just might make this unlikely hero the greatest ninja ever!
Naruto, vol. 1: Enter: Naruto
DVD in stores now!
SHONEN JUMP'S NARUTO
Enter:NARUTO
VOLUME 1
Enter:NARUTO
Complete your collection with NARUTO manga– buy volumes 1-9 at store.viz.com today!
Visit www.naruto.com for online games, downloads and more!
viz media
www.viz.com
© 2002 MASASHI KISHIMOTO Cover art subject to change.
DVD VIDEO
SHONEN JUMP
HOME VIDEO
www.shonenjump.com

It's the morning after an all-nighter. The hot, springtime sun burns into my eye sockets like fire. I stop my beloved car, City, beside a field and breathe the fresh, country air and the smell of grass into my nicotine-scarred lungs. Koff. Koff. A brownish-green blotch on one of my radials catches my eye—a lumpy, gooey thing with the texture of old hay. Why, it's a giant dog turd pressed deep into the tire grooves. *Yeaaaaargh!*

—Akira Toriyama, 1982

Akira Toriyama's first weekly series, **Dr. Slump**, has entertained generations of readers in Japan since it was introduced in Shueisha's **Weekly Shonen Jump** magazine in 1980. A few years later, he created his wildly popular **Dragon Ball** series, which brought him international success. Toriyama is also known for his character designs for video games, including **Dragon Warrior**, **Chrono Trigger** and **Tobal No. 1**. He lives with his family in Japan.

5-06
8⁰⁰

DR. SLUMP VOL. 7
The SHONEN JUMP Manga Edition

STORY AND ART BY
AKIRA TORIYAMA

English Adaptation & Translation/Alexander O. Smith
Touch-up Art & Lettering/Walden Wong
Cover & Interior Design/Hidemi Sahara
Editor/Yuki Takagaki

Managing Editor/Elizabeth Kawasaki
Director of Production/Noboru Watanabe
Vice President of Publishing/Alvin Lu
Vice President & Editor in Chief/Yumi Hoashi
Sr. Director of Acquisitions/Rika Inouye
Vice President of Sales & Marketing/Liza Coppola
Publisher/Hyoe Narita

Printed in the U.S.A.

Published by VIZ Media, LLC
P.O. Box 77010
San Francisco, CA 94107

SHONEN JUMP Manga Edition
10 9 8 7 6 5 4 3 2 1
First printing, May 2006

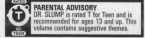

SHONEN JUMP MANGA

Dr. SLUMP™

Story & Art by

Akira Toriyama

DR. SLUMP Vol. 7

ACK! IT'S TIME FOR VOLUME 7 ALREADY? BUT I HAVE A...UH... HAIR APPOINTMENT! YEAH!
LAME...
CONTENTS

Witchey Gone Wild

TOO HOT!
IT'S HOT!
THUD-THUD-THUD
DING
CANNED FOOD
HOT HOT
BWEEEZ BWEEEZ

FLIT FLIT
BAKOOM!
HAYMAKER PUNCH!
PEE PEEE!
...
WA HA HA!
KOFF
SPLUNK
SNORT!

SILENCE, SILENCE, SILENCE!!
IT'S TOO HOT FOR SUCH MADNESS! TOO HOT!
HERE, HAVE A CREEMIE!
OH! OH HO HO...
PERHAPS I SHALL...
LICK LICK LICK
EH HEH HEH... ♡
YUMMY! HOW'D YOU MAKE THIS?
WELCOME TO "ARALE GETS COOKING"! FIRST, THE INGREDIENTS...
Creemie Mix
Milk
Gatchan
HUH? WHY GATCHAN...?

*FEED GATCHAN THE INGREDIENTS, THEN PLACE IN A MICROWAVE.

YAR!
YACK!
YAY!
SLURP
N'CHA!
YOU SCARED ME TO DEATH!!
YO!
MY SISTER'S COMIN' TODAY!
HUH!?
WELCOME!!
A CUTE IMP

VWOOOM
SNIK
VRRAAAW
ZING ZING
TAT-TAT

TINKLE
VWEEEEN
YEEARGH!
FWUP
WHEEE!
BTHOOM!
HO-YO...

TOUCHDOWN!
CRASH
ALLEY-OOP!
GREETINGS!
I'M CHIVIL'S OLDER SISTER, WITCHPEE!
ISN'T SHE SOMETHING?
N'CHA!
...
OH!
MY...
WHAT A HANDSOME FELLOW!

C'MON, SENBEI! YOU GOTTA ADMIT THAT'S THE FIRST TIME ANYONE'S *EVER* CALLED YOU HANDSOME!
DON'T TELL HER THAT!
IS YOUR SISTER'S HEAD ON RIGHT!?
WHAAA!? HUH!?
SO, HANDSOME, WHEN SHALL WE BE WED!?
I DON'T BELIEVE YOU.
COULD YOU... SAY THAT AGAIN?
HO HO!
D-DARLING...!?
OH?
MY, WHAT A DARLING LITTLE GIRL!
MAMAMA!
HUH?
AND YOU'LL BE THEIR UNCLE!
YOU CAN CALL ME "MAMA"!

"UNCLE"? WHY "UNCLE"?
AND AT THE TENDER AGE OF THREE. I SYMPATHIZE.
HO HO HO! SHALL I GIVE YOU A PIGGY-BACK RIDE, DEARIE?
UH HO HO HOY!
FWOMP
MMPH MMPH
HO-YO?
MY, MY!!
PUSHING YOUR MOTHER AROUND LIKE A TOY!
HEY, HONEY!!
C'MERE!
OH?
I'M OUTTA HERE!
BOMB!
VAKOOM
NOW, NOW, HONEY!

UH...
UH...
WHERE SHALL WE GO ON OUR SWEETEST OF HONEYMOONS!?
RELAX, SHE'S JUST A KID!
I KNOW!
I'LL BE FRANK, BUT KIND!
...MS. YAMABU...
HUH?
YES, I *AM* HANDSOME, PERHAPS EVEN *TOO* HANDSOME.
I CAN SEE HOW A GIRL MIGHT BE... TEMPTED.
HOWEVER, MY HEART BELONGS TO ANOTHER...

HOW MANY KIDS SHALL WE HAVE, HONEY?
WHAT?
PAPAPA!
DON'T EVER BRING HER HERE AGAIN!
GRR GRR
FWEEE
FWEEE
LEAVE ME ALONE!
MY!!
I LIKE THEM SLICK AND WELL GROOMED! ♡
H-HEY, LADY! I GOT A WIFE AND KIDS ALREADY...
WHEW!

Dad scolded me something crazy that night.

My Toilet Paper

1 Once upon a time there was a really rural town.

2 "Oh no, oh no, Mr. Mayor!"

3 "Yes, little Peasuke? Whatever is the matter?"

"It's horrible, sir. The town has run out of toilet paper."

"Out of toilet paper...? No-o-o-o..."

4 A town meeting was called to discuss the problem. "People, these are dire times. We must fix this problem, or stink. Some brave soul must offer to go to the super-market and buy more to-day. Who will it be?"

5 *Mutter, mutter.*
Whisper, whisper.

No one wants to go. Why? Because a horrible monster lives on the way to the super-market.

"Hey, Suppaman. You go. Aren't you the champion of justice?"

6 "I will not," said Suppaman bravely.

9 No one complained, though they had wished for a more dashing hero.

"Good luck, Senbei," said the Mayor, handing him a bag of coins.

"Heh heh heh. Leave it to me. This plane is my own design. I have nothing to fear."

7 Just then Akane spoke...

"Let's have the handsomest hero of all go."

It was a villager named Senbei who eagerly answered the call.

8 "What? You mean *I* have to go?"

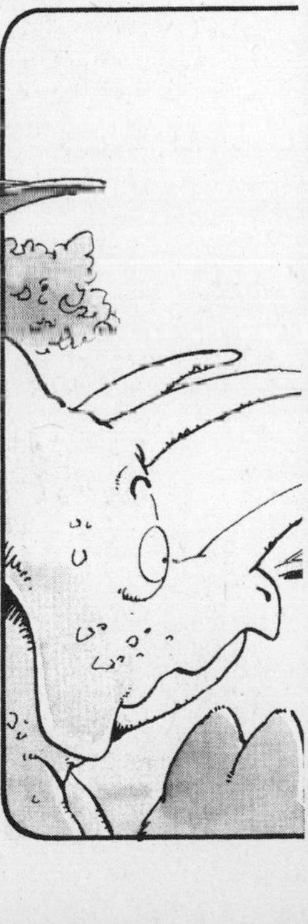

10 *Vroooom.*

"God speed. And come back quickly. We need to use the bath-room fast."

Senbei's air-plane zoomed into the sky, followed by the villagers' cheers.

11 *Splut splut.*
Vwooom.
Babooom.

The plane was soon grounded by engine trouble. "Owww."

12 "N'cha."

Two children appeared from no-where.

"Huh? What are you doing here?"

"We are Arale and Gatchan, friends to good little boys and girls every-where. Are you a good child?"

"Oh yes, I'm good."

13 "Ooh ho ho
h-o-o-y.
Then you are
our friend."

"Thank you."

And so
the three
headed off
to the
super-market
to-gether.

14 Soon they came
to a giant chasm.

"Wow, that's a
long way down."

"Ho-yo, that's a
long way down."

Gatchan
said nothing.

15 "Very well. I will show you how to jump. Watch what I do and follow. One, two, three..."
16 "Yeeaarrgh."
Senbei plummeted headlong down the chasm.
"Ho-yo. Interesting technique."
17 "Yeeaarrgh."
Arale watched what he did and followed.
18 "Wee hee. That was fun."
"Y-Yes. Fun. Ha ha."
Such good times, but just then...

19 "Rooooooooooooowrrr."
The terrible monster appeared with a horrible scream. This was his home.
"Yikes."

rrrrrrrr.
20 "Avast, monster. I will defeat you," said Senbei, bravely drawing his sword.
BOTE!!
22 He lost.
23 "Mmmmph. I'm not through with you."
Senbei dusted himself off and stood up.

21 Harrrrrr
21 The monster was Arale's pet.
Shake.
SSA
DEN!

25 After crossing a treacherous mountain pass, the intrepid band finally arrived at a lighted store-house.

"It's the super-market."

26 "Is anyone home?"

Senbei called out with his last remaining strength.

27 "Welcome to our store." Inside was the beautifulest woman Senbei had ever seen.

1520
60% OFF!
28 "Oh ho ho. Shopping are we? How may I help you?"
29 "Please make me your boy-friend!" "Certainly, sir."
PICTURE BOOK
30 And so, though it boggles the mind, the two were wed and lived happily ever after. Congratulations!
I'm gonna do it! I'm gonna use the leaf!
Where is that Senbei!?
TOILET
THE END

The things we try to forget...
The Non-Fiction Theater's
ME BACK THEN REDUX
2 A MIDSUMMER NIGHT'S MYSTERY
This tale also took place in elementary school. One steamy night, as I was walking home...
La la...
...I came across a large rock on the ground.
Huh?
I had an urge to throw it, so I picked it up and hurled it into the darkness.
Yar!
Then, from the darkness I heard...
YEARGH!
...a voice! Wondering what it was, I walked in that direction...
The boy next door was lying on the ground. His head was bleeding.
What happened?
S-Something c-came flying!
Next to him lay the stone that I had thrown.
Dad scolded me something fierce that night.
No throwing stones in the dark!

Mister Copy
Mister Copy
Mister Copy

BRUSH BRUSH
BRUSH BRUSH
RINSE, THEN TALK!
DOGTOR! DOGTOR!
SPIF SPIF
GARGLE GARGLE
GARGLE GARGLE
USE A TOWEL!
WIPEY WIPE
WIPE WIPE
WHO!

READ THIS WAY

STRETCH
AHH!
BRRING BRRING
HUH?
BRRRING BRRRING
HEY! PHONE! PICK ME UP!
FINE, FINE!
HULLO?
NORIMAKI SPEAK-ING...
THIS IS MS. YAMABUKI. SORRY TO CALL SO LATE...
M-M-MS. YAMABUKI!?

READ THIS WAY
WOOO! WOOO!
UM, ACTUALLY, I HAVE TWO TICKETS TO A MATINEE.
AND I WAS WONDERING... IF YOU'RE NOT BUSY, WOULD YOU LIKE TO GO TOMORROW?
TOMORROW!? I'M NOT BUSY TOMORROW! NOT AT ALL!!!
O-OH, I SEE, WELL...
HOW ABOUT TOMORROW MORNING, 10 O'CLOCK...?
DING
OOF...
GRIN

WHOOPEE! WHOOPEE!
AT LAST! AT LAST!
WHOOP! WOO...
OH NO! THE AMUSEMENT PARK!
WE'LL GO ANOTHER DAY. THEY'LL UNDERSTAND.
OH, ARALE! GATCHAN!
EXCUSE ME! ♡
Y'KNOW... ♡
BANG
CRASH
WHEE HEE HEE!

READ THIS WAY

COCK-A-OODLE-OOH
YAWN...
DIT DIT DIT
SKREE SKREE
DONG DONG
BANG BANG
LATE NIGHT, HUH?
I'VE MADE MR. COPY!
I DID IT!
COPY
HUFF
HUFF
FINE. VERY WELL.
C'MON, C'MON, C'MON!
SO INFANTILE...
ALL RIGHT! GET TO WORK! I NEED ANOTHER ME!
IT'S BEEN WHILE SINCE YOUR LAST INVENTION. WHY DON'T YOU EXPLAIN HOW I WORK TO EVERYONE?

HERE GOES! READY?
AND... CHEESE!
SNAP
IT WORKED!
NNGH!
SPUT
GET GOING!
NO WAY! I'M GOING OUT WITH MIDORI!
WHAT!?
OKAY, YOU'RE TAKING ARALE TO THE PARK!
HUH?
...
COPY
OH YEAH, PIG FACE!?
OH YEAH, RUNT LEGS!?
SMACK
SMACK
SMACK
YOU BETTER WATCH WHO YOU'RE MESSING WITH!

I'M GOING TO THE MOVIE, AND THAT'S FINAL!
HUFF
HUFF
HUFF
HUFF
HUFF
I'LL SHOW YOU WHAT'S FINAL!
HUFF
GRR...
PICK PICK
YAR!
FWIP
SMACK
ACK!
SENBEI!! COME BACK HERE, YOU IDIOT!
LEAVE ME ALONE, JERK!
TUT TUT TUT
OH NO. OH DEAR.
COPY
I'VE COPIED AN IDIOT.

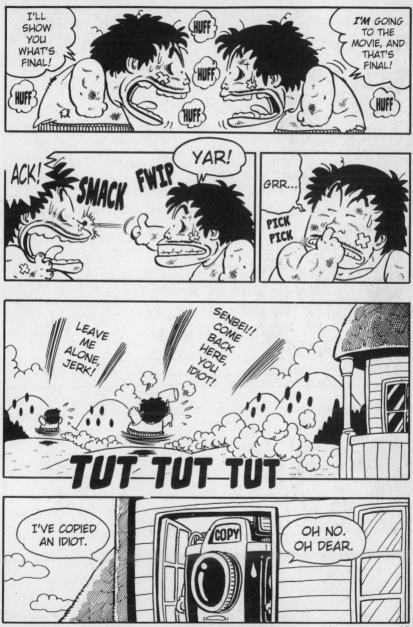

VWIP
A-YA-YA?
VWIP
LET'S GO, DOCTOR!
HO-YO!?
WHO'RE YOU?
GREETINGS. I AM MR. COPY.
FLIT FLIT
ARE YOU STRONG?
NOT STRONG, BUT I CAN DO AN AMAZING TRICK!

LEMME SEE! LEMME SEE!
VERY WELL...
PLEASE, STAND OVER THERE.
YOU DUMMY! LOOK AT ALL THE TIME YOU'VE WASTED!
ME!? ME!? YOU'RE THE ONE...!

READ THIS WAY

The things we try to forget...
The Non-Fiction Theater's
ME BACK THEN REDUX
3 LEADERSHIP AND DOGGIE POOP
Our tale begins one fine day during a walk...
YES, LEADER!
Follow me, scouts!
When I was young all the neighborhood kids were smaller than me, which made me bold.
As ill luck would have it, I sat right down on the turd, and it stuck.
ACK!
BWA HA HA!
I stepped on a turd and slipped.
YEEARGH!
FWIP
That night those cheeky boys told their parents, and my dad bawled me out.
BONK
WAAAAH
BONK
WAAAAH
Shut up!
My rep as leader was destroyed. The other kids just laughed. That made me mad.

Vacuum 1982

BADABADA
WREEEORW
VMM
VMM
SPEED LIMIT 50
DOO DOO
DA
DOO DOO
DOO DOO DA
DOO DOO DA
VMMM
VA VA
AHH...
WHO'S NEXT...?
STORMY WAY, NUMBER 8, EH?

Vacuum
1982

VAC
PENGUIN
62-15
DONK
DONK
DONK
VWEEEE
SHUPOK
PENGUIN
VILLAGE
VACUUM CA

QUITE A BUILD-UP YOU'VE GOT HERE.
I CAN'T THANK YOU ENOUGH!
VZZORP
FWOP
VUDVUDVUDVUD
BRRRRUN
I BROUGHT YOU A SNACK. I'LL LEAVE IT HERE FOR WHEN YOU'RE DONE.
THANKS.
IT'S CURRY...
VWOOOOM
ZUPZUPZUP
FWRRR
JUST A LITTLE MORE!
HUH!?

READ THIS WAY

WALK THE POOP!!
FWAP
YAR!
CH-CHEEKY!
VWOOM
HA HA! POOP HEADS!!
HEH HEH! YOU LIKE THAT!?
WHA...!?

AAAARGH!!
KIIIIN
FWAP
SUCH MAD-NESS!
VACUUUUUUUM
SPEED METER

160
170
190
T-TWO HUNDRED MILES PER HOUR!?
ZOIK
HEH HEH! HOW'D YOU LIKE THAT!?
AAAAGH!
TH-THAT'S IMPOSSIBLE!!!

READ THIS WAY
HUH!?
CLIFF AHEAD. WATCH OUT!
A-HA! I KNOW!
VROOM
SPLASHHH
HO-YO!

WOOOOOOH
BLUB
BLUB
PENGUIN VILLAGE VACUUM CAR
PENGUIN 62-15
WHEW...
DIDN'T SEE THAT COMING, DID YOU?
IT'S A REMORA SHARK!

READ THIS WAY

BWOOSH
PENGUIN VILLAGE
VWEEEEN
WHEW...
IT'S OVER. IT'S ALL OVER.
NOW I JUST HAVE TO FINISH THE VACUUMING.
THAT WAS QUITE THE DETOUR...
LET'S SEE...
FLIT FLIT

FIRE MISSILES!!
BZZZZZAP
BTHOOOOOOOM!!
BYE'CHA!
TWITCH
TWITCH
I, TOO, SPENT MY YOUTH CHASING THE VACUUM CAR.
- THE AUTHOR

FREEBIE
☆Deluxe Special ☆
Dress-Me Nikochan
Nikochan is naked and abashed! Dress him as you like.
Tee hee! Make me look good! ♡
SNEAKERS for growing boys
GLOVES
BOOTS
BRA I'm a grown-up, you know. ♥
DRESS for when you feel like a grown-up.
SEXY PANTIES
FASHIONABLE SHADES
FASHIONABLE HAT for shade in the hot summer sun.
HIGH HEELS If you don't have good shoes, you have nothing.
KNIT VEST and WRAPAROUND SKIRT for a casual look.

Goo Ga Senbei

WHEW
SNUFF
STRETCH
YOUNG

READ THIS WAY

I'M GETTING OLD!
OLD AGE!
NO MATTER HOW HANDSOME THEY MIGHT BE!
I DON'T LIKE OLD MEN!
QUICK!
MUST MAKE YOUTH SERUM!!
KIIIN!
OH NO-O-O-O!
YOUNG
YOUNG

MILK
MILK
WORM EYES (3 PCS.)
DRIED PLUMS (3 PCS.)
GAMERA EGGS (2 PCS.)
SUGAR CUBES (1.5 PCS.)
SALT (1 TBSP.)
ENERGY DRINK (1 BOTTLE)
MIX INGREDIENTS WELL IN A BOWL, HEAT ON A LOW FLAME FOR 20 MINUTES, THEN LET COOL.
IT'S DONE!!!
TO YOUTH!
MMMK.
MMMK.
HIK
HIK
KOFF
HIK
HIK

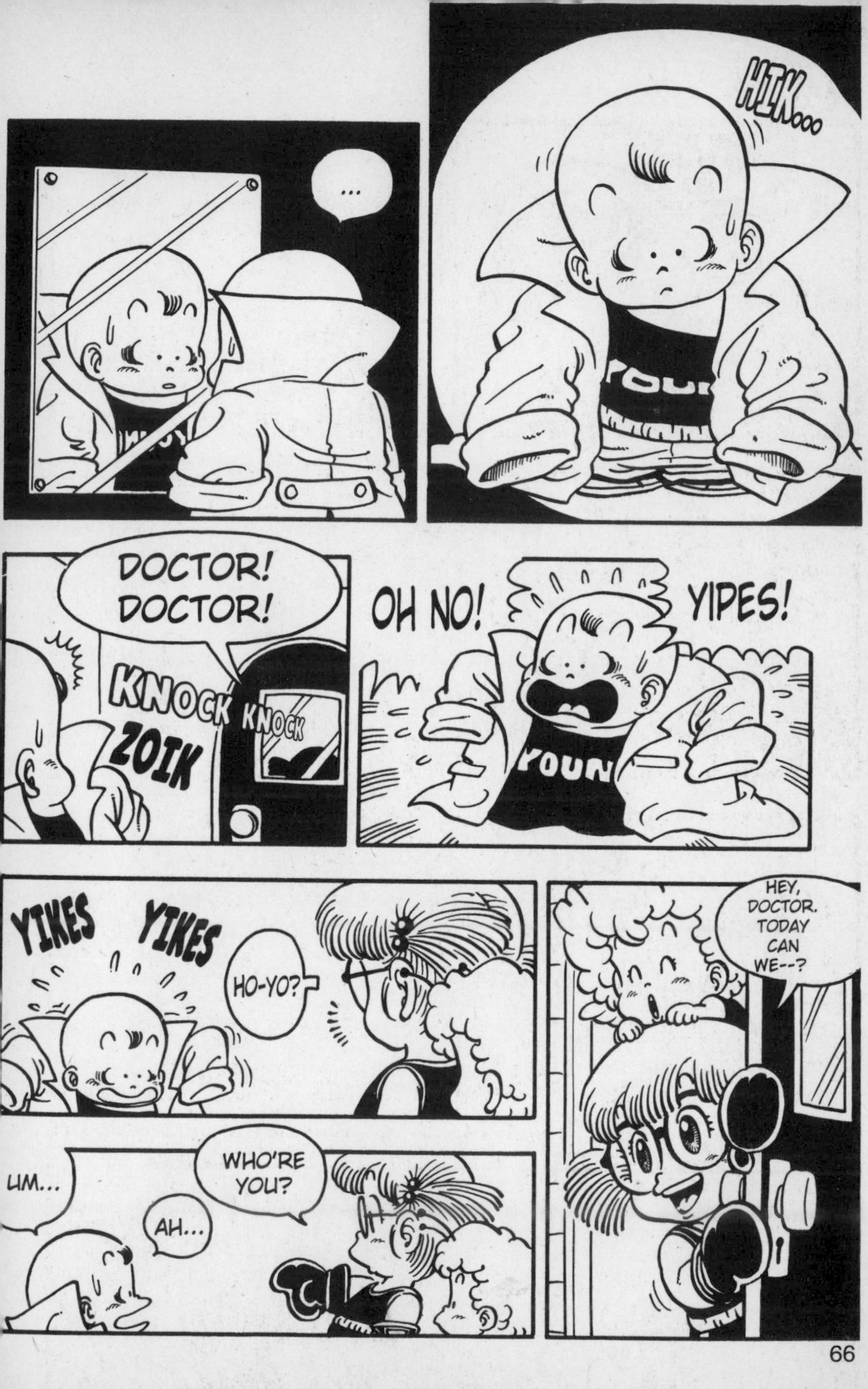
HIK...
...
OH NO!
YIPES!
DOCTOR! DOCTOR!
KNOCK KNOCK
ZOIK
HEY, DOCTOR. TODAY CAN WE--?
YIKES YIKES
HO-YO?
WHO'RE YOU?
AH...
UM...

READ THIS WAY
I-I'M A KID.
OH.
KNOW WHERE THE DOCTOR IS?
UH... UM...
WONDER WHERE HE WENT.
MS. YAMABUKI'S COMING OVER...
WHA--!?
FOR REAL, ARALE!?
SHE'S REALLY COMING!? HERE!?
YIPPEE! YIPPEE!
HO-YO...
ACK!
OH NO!
BING BONG
WAAAAH! WAAAAH!
THAT'S HER!

SO SENBEI ISN'T HERE?
I BROUGHT GROCERIES FOR DINNER.
YEAH!
IT'LL WEAR OFF EVENT-UALLY.
OH WELL...
'OUNG
I'LL SURPRISE HIM!
HO HO!
GUESS I'LL JUST MAKE IT WHILE HE'S OUT.
THIS'LL BE YUMMY!
YAY!
HUH?
MIDORI-I-I-I!!!
MI...
!!

READ THIS WAY

HAW
DUMB
M 78
SENBEI SURE IS LATE...
WONDER WHAT HE'S DOING.
MUNCH MUNCH
...
GA GA GOO GOO!
EH?
BOOBY!
BOO!

READ THIS WAY
WHAT? OH, DO YOU WANT TO NURSE?
YAH!
YAH!
HERE!
FWOMP
WHO THE HECK WANTS TO SEE THAT!?
THAT'S FINE. REALLY!
I'M SORRY, BUT THAT ISN'T POSSIBLE.
...
DARN IT!
A-HA!
GRIIIN
BA-BA-BATH!
EH?

HURRY!
HURRY!
WHOSE BABY IS THIS?
BRA, BRA!
ZOING
HUFF!
HUFF!
I SAW HER BOOBIES!
AMAZING! SIMPLY AMAZING!
I CAN DIE FULFILLED!
BUT I DON'T WANT TO DIE.
IN ALL THEIR GLORY!
SPLURRRT
SPOO
SPOO
SPOO
SPOO

EEEK! OH NO!
HE SANK!
IN BED WITH MIDORI! IT'S LIKE A DREAM COME TRUE!
ARE YOU OKAY?
O-OH YEAH.
VWOP
GOTTA MIL
THIS FOR A
IT'S WORTH!
DR. SLUMP...
FIND IT IN THE OCCULT MANGA SECTION.
YEEEEARGH!!!

Dr. Slump SUPER Quiz

♡ Penguin Village Daycare Entrance Exam

Part One

If any of the following statements is true, fill in the corresponding box under the O in the answers section below. If it's not true, fill in the box under the X.

1. Sure, Arale's human.
2. Arale's wicked weak.
3. Arale's got wicked good eyesight.
4. Gatchan can fly.
5. Senbei likes to read dirty magazines.
6. Taro and Peasuke are father and son.
7. Suppaman's dumb.
8. King Nikochan's an Earthling. Yeah.
9. What do you find on the ground in Penguin Village? Answer: Poop.
10. Penguin Village is so peaceful, they don't need any police.

Part Two

Read the following questions (1-5) very carefully. Choose your answers from A, B, or C and place a check mark in the appropriate box below.

1. What is Arale's hobby?
   A. Cooking
   B. Sewing
   C. Poop poking

2. How does Gatchan say "hello"?
   A. Zoo Pee Pee
   B. Koo Pee Pee
   C. Ho Hya Hya

3. Who stole Senbei's heart?
   A. Kinoko Sarada
   B. Old woman Spring
   C. Midori Yamabuki

4. What business runs out of Taro's house?
   A. Barbershop
   B. Green grocer
   C. Toy store

5. What delicious food did Bubibinman find on Earth?
   A. Carrots
   B. Poop
   C. Spinach

Answers on page 194.

Answer Sheet: Use a No. 2 pencil!

[Part One] 5 Points

	○ ✕		○ ✕		○ ✕		○ ✕		○ ✕
1.	□□	2.	□□	3.	□□	4.	□□	5.	□□
6.	□□	7.	□□	8.	□□	9.	□□	10.	□□

[Part Two] 10 Points

	A B C		A B C		A B C		A B C		A B C
1.	□□□	2.	□□□	3.	□□□	4.	□□□	5.	□□□

Name		Birth date	Year of Birth: [ ] [ ] [ ][ ] Month: [ ] Box Pufferfish [ ] Crayfish [ ] Coelacanth [ ] Plankton [ ] Puffer Fish Day: [ ][ ]	Points	

The Biggest Bye'cha of All
Part One

VS

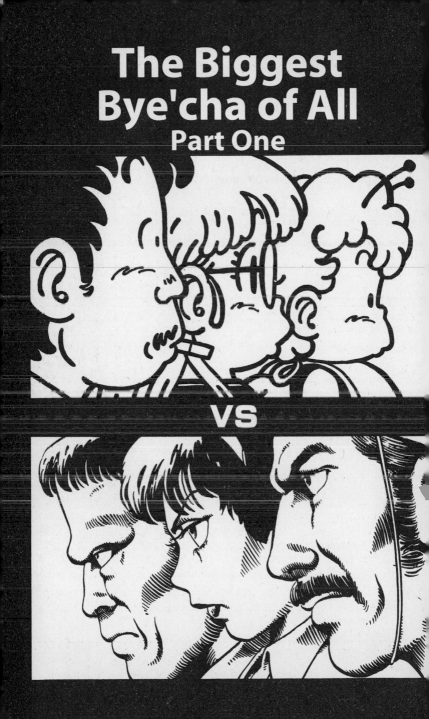

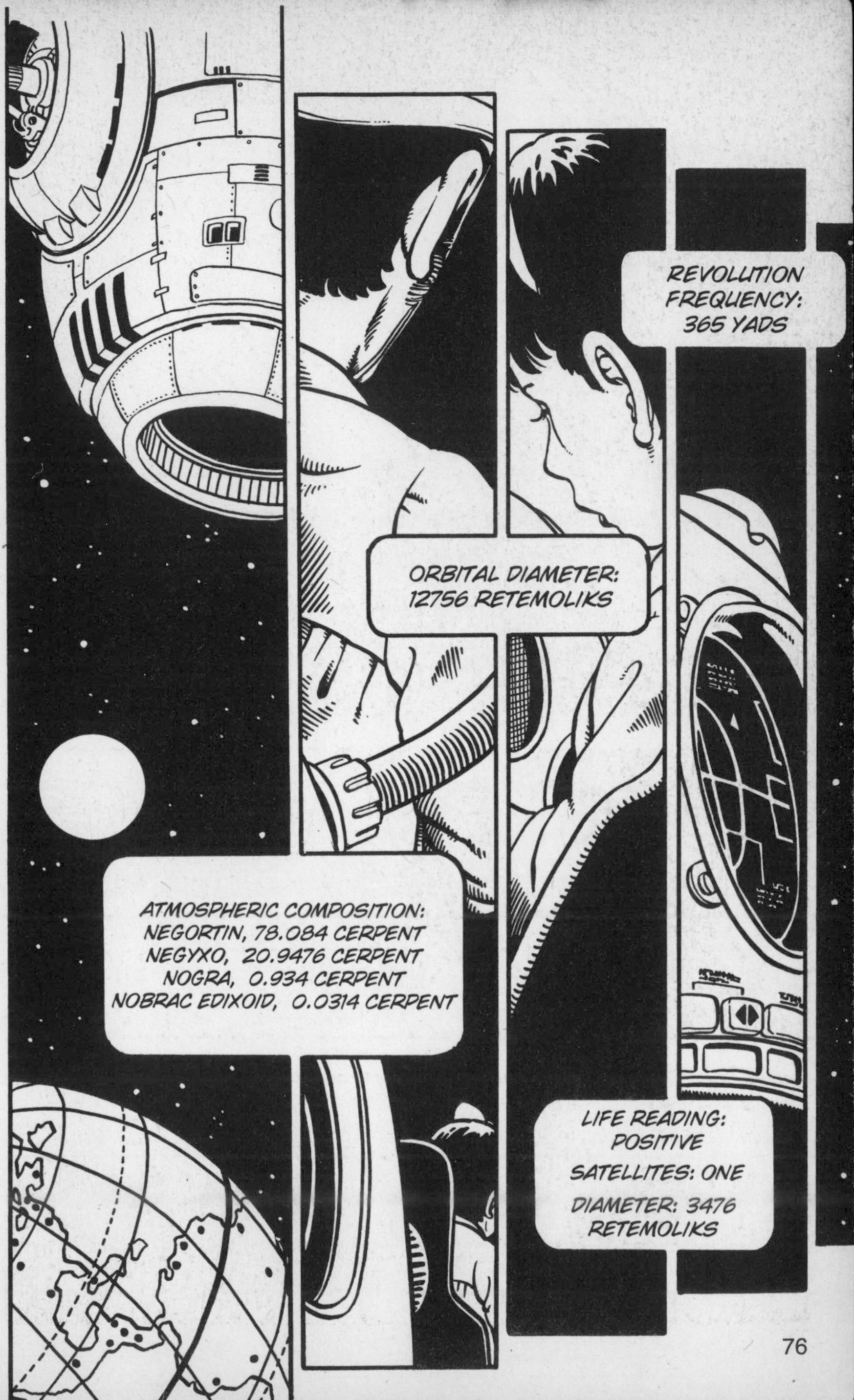
REVOLUTION FREQUENCY: 365 YADS
ORBITAL DIAMETER: 12756 RETEMOLIKS
ATMOSPHERIC COMPOSITION:
NEGORTIN, 78.084 CERPENT
NEGYXO, 20.9476 CERPENT
NOGRA, 0.934 CERPENT
NOBRAC EDIXOID, 0.0314 CERPENT
LIFE READING: POSITIVE
SATELLITES: ONE
DIAMETER: 3476 RETEMOLIKS

EXCELLENT!
THIS IS THE IDEAL PLANET.
SENDING SPYBALL.
SEARCH FOR INTELLIGENT LIFE FORMS AND STUDY THEIR CIVILIZATION!

VWOOOM
PHUT
VERY WELL. KEEP MONITORING!
SIR!
WHAT STRANGE LIFE FORMS ARE ON THIS PLANET!
LET'S LOOK AROUND, SHALL WE?

READ THIS WAY

FLIK
ACH!
RIDIC-ULOUS...
WHY, THAT IMPERTINENT LITTLE LIFE FORM!
YAARGH YAARGH
IT REMOVED ITS OWN HEAD! FASCINATING!
HUFF
HUFF
HUFF

WEEN WEEN
BEEP BEEP
ENOUGH OF THE LOCAL LIFE FORMS! LET'S EXAMINE THEIR CIVILIZATION.
AT ONCE, SIR.
PHUT
LOOK! LOOK! TIRES! THEY'RE STILL USING TIRES!!
THAT'S MORE PRIMITIVE THAN ANYTHING WE HAVE ON RECORD! HOW UNCIVILIZED...
NYAH.
ARALE

WE'RE GONNA HAVE AN INVASION!
THIS PLANET IS OURS! WHOOPEE!
CHOOL! PRES CHOOL! ARE YOU READY!?
YES, SIR!
NOW! RELEASE THE MOBILE SUIT THAT'S POPULAR WITH THE KIDS!
DESTROY ALL LIFE AND ALL VESTIGES OF CIVILIZATION ON THE PLANET! MAKE IT CLEAN!
YES, BOSS!
WHEW. FOR A MINUTE THERE I THOUGHT HE'D MAKE ME GO DOWN AND DO IT MYSELF.

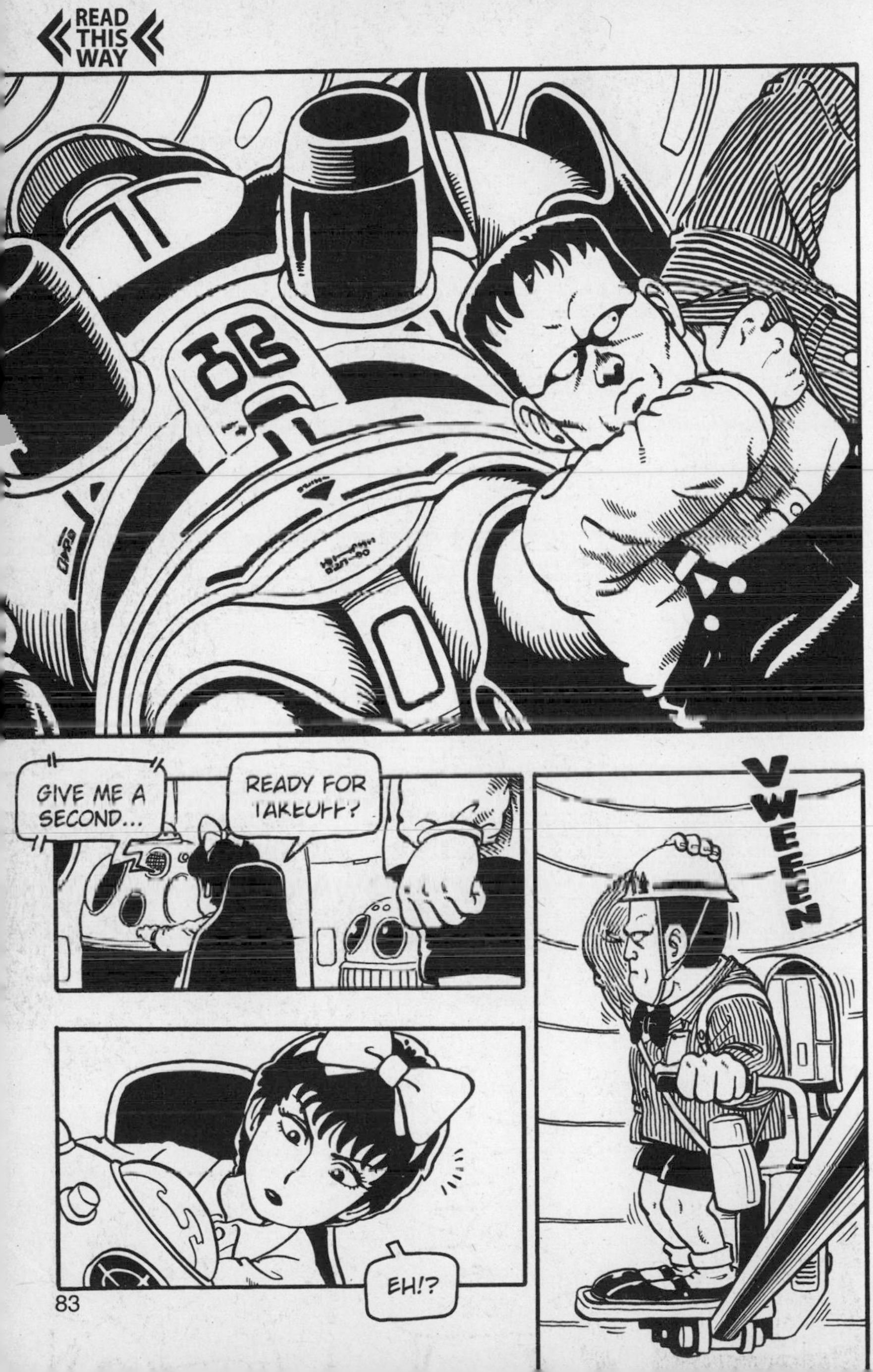
READ THIS WAY
VWEEEN
READY FOR TAKEOFF?
GIVE ME A SECOND...
EH!?

*THE WORD FOR "POOP" ON THEIR PLANET. (BY THE WAY, "PEE" IS "DONWETYERPANTS.")

WEEEN
BOM!
BONK
HA HA! TAKE THAT!
HO-YO...
WHAT'S WRONG, RIBBONGIRL?
MMMP
FFFFFFP
FFFFP
LOOK, SIR. I DESTROYED ONE.

N'CHAAAAAA
BAKOOM!
Oh, n'cha, bye'cha! N'cha, bye'cha! Arale goes bye'cha! Ha ha ha!
HMM? I CAN'T SEE ANYTHING.
WHAT!?
THAT'S ODD. I WONDER WHAT'S WRONG.
A CAMERA MAL-FUNCTION, PERHAPS?
BLOOP BLOOP
THIS IS CHOOL. READY FOR TAKE OFF!

BYE-BYE, MOBILE SUIT "ROCKCOACH"!
LAUNCH! DO YOUR THING!
ROGER!
I'M ON MY WAY!
He's taking off...to destroy the world!
It's evil Mobile Suit Rockcoach!
Will Earth live to see tomorrow!?
Will Dr. Slump continue!?
Yes, it will! To be continued!

The Biggest Bye'cha of All
Part Two

HE'S HERE! THE BIGGEST, EVILEST ALIEN MOBILE SUIT OF ALL..."ROCKCOACH"!
UH-OH! BYE'CHA, EARTH! WAIT! I STILL HAVEN'T DONE EVERYTHING I WANTED TO DO!
GUAAAAAA!!
SHOW NO MERCY! KILL AT WILL! GO WILD!
PREPARING FOR LANDING. SWITCHING TO ATTACK FORMATION.
SAFETY FIRST
MILK
25¢

DODODOOOOOO
KIIIIN
ARALE
SCREEE
ALE
HO-YO-YO-YO-YO?

SAFETY FIRST
MWAH HA HA! HEEEEEERE'S ROCKCOACH!

HACHINK
COFFEE
Pot
A-YA-YA!?
EAT THIS! IT'S A BLAST FROM MY ROCKCOACH HYPER DDT BAZOOKA!
25¢
HO-YO! THAT'S COOL!!
ARALE

READ THIS WAY

WON!
TOO!
TREE!
TAP
TAP
WHEE HEE! I WON! I WON!
BYE'CHA!
UNNNNH... UNNGH
!?
TH-THAT'S ODD... MASTER KIN DER GARTEN!
WE'VE LOST THE SIGNAL!
WHAT!?

READ THIS WAY

HEY, CHOOL! PRES CHOOL! WHAT'S WRONG? DO YOU READ!? ANSWER ME!
BLAST! THE TRANSMITTER'S DOWN! I CAN'T SEE ANYTHING!
OH NO, MY SCENES OF DESTRUCTION...!
GAN!
WE'LL JUST HAVE TO WITNESS THEM FIRST-HAND!
WHAT'S TAKING ARALE SO LONG?
SHE'S GOOFING OFF AGAIN ON THE WAY HOME!
KOO POO!
HUH!?

HEY, THAT'S MY GOOD OLD BIG-SMALL RAY GUN!
THAT'S NOT A TOY. GIVE IT HERE...
BIIIIG
CRAK
SNAP
SHOULD BE AROUND HERE...
DODOOOOO..!!

AAAH!
VZZZ...
ROCKCOACH HAS FALLEN!! HE'S OVER THERE, ON THE RIGHT!
WHAAAT!?
TUT TUT TUT
ARE YOU OKAY!? WHAT HAPPENED?
I-I DUNNO... IT ALL HAPPENED SO QUICKLY.
DOM DOM DOM

YOU COME BACK HERE, GATCHAN!!!
...
WAIT UP!!
DOM DOM DOM
...
...
YEEEEEAAAAARGH!

FLIT FLIT
GIVE IT BACK!!
!!
DOM DOM DOM
THAT WAS CLOSE!
YIPES! IT'S A PLANET OF GIANTS!
AND SO THE NORIMAKIS SAVED THE EARTH. AGAIN.

Penguin Village Dom-Dom-Dom!

READ THIS WAY

YEEEAARRRGH! IT'S THE HO-YO-YO GIRL AND THE KOO-PEE-PEE KID!!!
HO-YO-YO!!!
KOO PEE PEE!
IT'S BEEN SO LONG I LET MY GUARD DOWN! OH NO! OUR SHIP IS SUNK! WE'RE DOOMED!
RUN AWAY!
SCREEEEE
NO-O-O! THEY'RE GAINING!
HO-YO-YO!

HO-YO-YO!
KOO PEE PEE!
!!
THEY DIDN'T DO ANYTHING!
HOW CAN THAT BE?
...
WHY DOES IT FEEL LIKE SOME-THING TERRIBLE IS ABOUT TO HAPPEN?
SEE HOW TIGHTLY SHE GRIPS THAT BAG! I WONDER WHAT'S INSIDE...
WAIT A SECOND...
WEE-OOH
WEE-OOH
QUICK! FOLLOW THEM... AND DON'T LET THEM SEE US!
HO-YO! HO-YO!
KOO PEE! KOO PEE!
POLICE
POLICE
SUBARU

VOOOO
WEE-OOH
WEE-OOH
WHAT'S GOING ON OVER THERE!?
WHOA WHOA
THAT WAS ARALE AND GATCHAN IN FRONT!
WEE-OOH
HO-YO! HO-YO!
DON'T YOU KNOW? SOMETHING TERRIBLE'S GOING TO HAPPEN! IN OTHER WORDS, WORLDWIDE DESTRUCTION!
WHAT!?
I'LL GO CHECK IT OUT!
VWOOOON
LET'S CHECK IT OUT.
WAAAH!? THAT'S HUGE!
HEY, THEY SAY THE WORLD IS ENDING!

READ THIS WAY

POLICE

READ THIS WAY

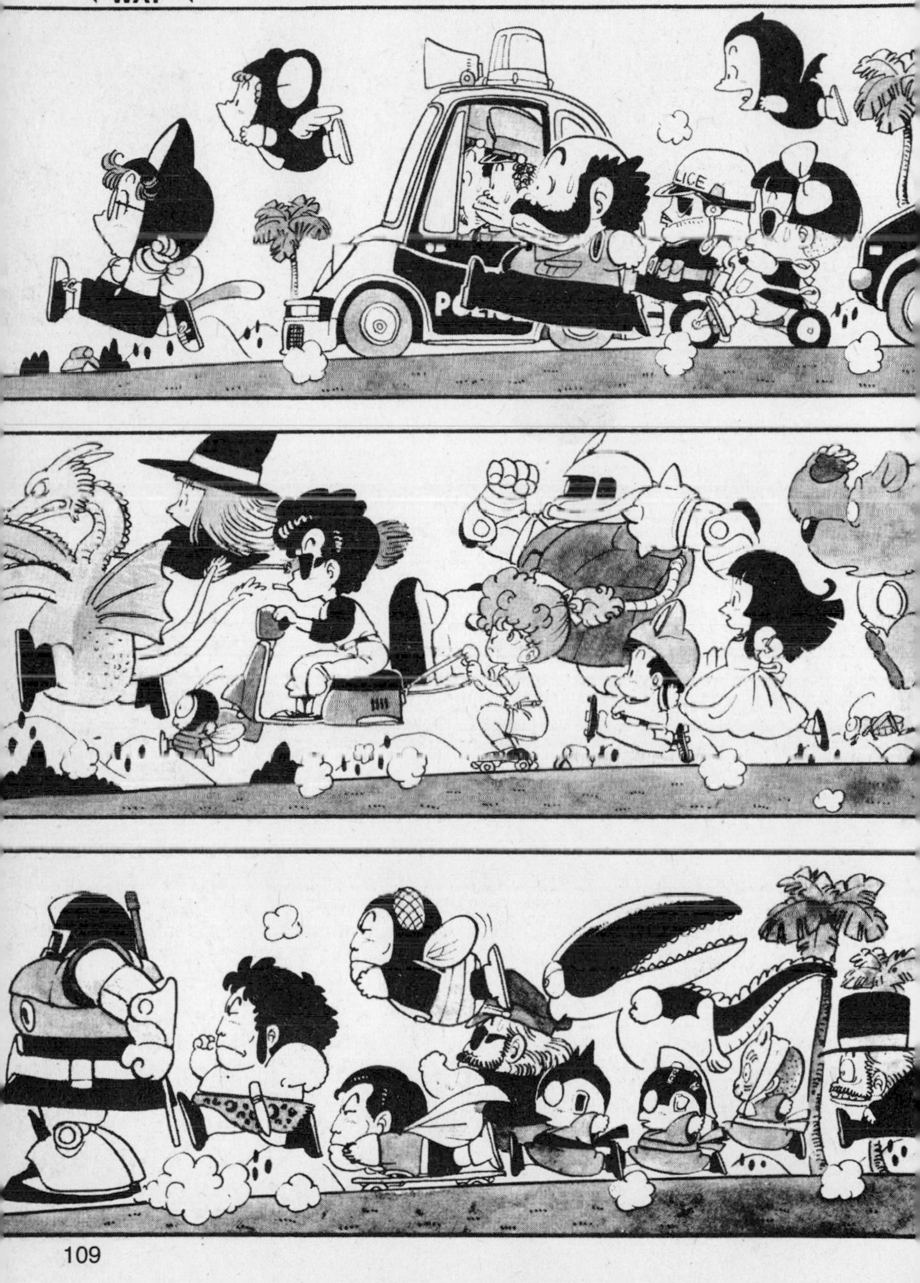

DOM DOM DOM DOM
FASTER!
A-YA-YA!
DRIP DRIP
ACK!
VWEEEEEN
KIIIIN
POLICE
WAIT, DON'T STOP THE CAR!
DARN IT! AFTER WE'VE COME ALL THIS WAY!
WE LOST THEM.
WHA...?

READ THIS WAY
STOP HERE AND WE'LL BE TRAMPLED TO DEATH!
DOM DOM DOM
OKAY. LET'S KEEP DRIVING UNTIL THEY LEAVE.
DOCTOR! I'M BACK!
MY ICE CREAM! IT DIDN'T MELT, DID IT!?
ONLY A LITTLE!
WOO HOO!
LICK LICK
EH HEH HEH!
THAT EVENING...
DOM DOM DOM DOM
ZZZ ZZZ
ZZZ ZZZ
WHAT'S ALL THE RUCKUS? IT'S THE MIDDLE OF THE NIGHT!
THREE DAYS LATER...
WEEE-OOOH WEEE-OOOH
WOBBLE WOBBLE
WHY'RE WE STILL RUNNING?
HUFF
LURCH LURCH
HUFF

Stone Age Ho-Yo-Yo

COCK-A-DOODLE-WHEE
YAAAAWN.
OOP! OOOOP!
SKOOL LATE! SKOOL LATE!

MMPH. MRR.
YAAWN.
MORNIN'. MORNIN'.
MORNIN'. MORNIN'.
MORNIN'. MORNIN'.
KOOPEEPEE. KOOPEEPEE.
HO-YO-YO? GLASSES...
CAVEMEN GLASSES NO-NO!
BYE'CHA-CHA!
FUN YOU HAVE!
ALLEY-OOP!

READ THIS WAY

*ARALE-ISM FOR "COOL."

READ THIS WAY

PHUT
OOOG! ARALE! HELP!
YUP YUP!
CLAP CLAP CLAP CLAP
ARALE GOOD! ARALE GOOD! CLAP CLAP!
CLAP
FWAAH
YEEARGHH!!
OOG?
WHAT WRONG?

HO-YO!?
SNAK
AAAACH!
HAVE FUN! PANTIES!
OH NO NO!
OOOG! TEACHER! TEACHER!

OOG OOG OOG! TEACHER! TEACHER!
WOOGA! ME USE THIS!
KACHAK
OOOG! THAT! WHAT WHAT!?
THIS WATER GUN.
IDIOT!
EEEK! WHAT YOU DO!? I CALL POLICE! POLICE!
LEMME GO, YOU!
WAA! WAA!
TEACHER!

READ THIS WAY

HEH HEH HEH.
BARURU BURURUU...
GENIUS! GEEEENIUS! BWA HA HA!
YES, SIR! THIS IS OUR CHANCE!
WE'LL WIN FOR SURE!
LOOK! PRIMITIVES!
GAN!
HUH?

ACK!
AYEEEEEEEE!
OOOG!
TEACHER!!!
TRIP
...
TOO BAD.
TOO BAD.
TWITCH
TWITCH

Dr. Slump SUPER Quiz

♡ Penguin Village Elementary School Entrance Exam

Part One

If any of the following statements is true, fill in the corresponding box under the O in the answers section below. If it's not true, fill in the box under the X.

1. Arale's good at removing her head.
2. Arale and Akane are in the same grade.
3. Gatchan was born from an egg.
4. Penguin Village is on Mizusumashi Island.
5. Kinoko Sarada's trademark is her bowl haircut.
6. Suppaman came from planet Okaka-umeboshi.
7. Dr. Mashirito is a benevolent, outstanding scientist.
8. The sun in Penguin Village is wicked bright.
9. Ms. Yamabuki has been seen wearing hippo panties; it's true!
10. Arale wears pumpkin panties.

Part Two

Read the following questions (1-5) very carefully. Choose your answers from A, B, or C and place a check in the appropriate box below.

1. What's Arale's best subject?
   A. Math
   B. Japanese
   C. Social Studies

2. What business does Akane's family run?
   A. A restaurant
   B. A café
   C. A department store

3. What is Peasuke's hobby?
   A. Stamp collecting
   B. Turd collecting
   C. Autograph collecting

4. What crafty fox lives in Penguin Village?
   A. Gon
   B. Donbe
   C. Bagone

5. What is Suppaman's secret weapon?
   A. His beloved triangular ruler
   B. His feared lower lip
   C. His courageous pointer finger

Answers on page 194.

Answer Sheet: Use a No. 2 pencil!

[Part One] 5 Points

	○×	○×	○×	○×	○×
	1. □□	2. □□	3. □□	4. □□	5. □□
	6. □□	7. □□	8. □□	9. □□	10. □□

[Part Two] 10 Points

A B C	A B C	A B C	A B C	A B C
1. □□□	2. □□□	3. □□□	4. □□□	5. □□□

Name		Birth date	Penguin Village, Gengoro Island [ ] Platypus [ ] Flying Squirrel [ ] Armadillo Apt. no. [ ][ ]	Points	

FOR DUMB KIDS WHO DON'T KNOW "CINDERELLA."

So, like, Cinderella was always, like, getting picked on by her step mom and her mean sisters, y'know? So then there was this, like, dance party at the local palace, and she, like, didn't have a dress so she couldn't go. But she had this Fairy Godmother who, like, gave her this dress and so then she goes and, like, marries a prince, right? Like, y'know? No? Oh.

Some characters and content in this story may have been changed from the original. Thank you for your cooperation.

WON.
TOO.
UH WON.
TOO.
TREE.
FOR.
A LONG, LONG TIME AGO-O-O...
WOO YEAAAH!
...WHO LIVED TOGETHER WITH A CUTE GIRL!
THERE WAS AN EVIL STEPMOM AND HER DAUGHTERS...
IT'S "CINDERELLA"!
WHAT'S HER NAME? WHAT'S HER NAME?

READ THIS WAY

PINS, FROM RIGHT TO LEFT: "SU" FOR SUPPAMAN," "MA" FOR "MASHIRITO" AND "PA" FOR PARZAN."

READ THIS WAY

DRESS-UP! ♪
MAKE-UP! ♪
THE DANCE IS TODAY! THE DAAAAANCE! ♫
HITCHED-UP! ♪
GET HITCHED! ♫
♫ CATCH HIS EYE, THE EYE OF THE PRIIIIINCE! ♪
YOODOO-LAY HEEHOO! YOODOO-LAY HEEHOO! ♫
YOU STAY HOME, CINDERELLA! ♫
WHAT FREAKS...

READ THIS WAY

I'M OVER HERE!! ♫
THERE SHE IS! THERE SHE IS! ♪ YOO HOO HOO!
CRASH
WHAM
PH-P-HUT
PHUT PHUT
WOO... ♪
UNH...
WOO HOO!
...
MAKE ME PRETTY, FAIRY GODMOTHER! PRETTY, PRETTY PLEEEEASE! ♫
SHE'LL BE HERE SOON! I KNOW! ♪
JUST A MISTAKE! A SIMPLE MISTAAAAKE! ♫
HOO HOO! ♪

GAN!
!!
NNNGRAH!
OH!
MY FAIRY GODMOTHER!
N'CHAAAAA!

HERE YOU GO-O-O!
WHAT COULD IT BE?
I KNOW! I KNOW! IT'S A DRESS!
WHEE WHEE!
POOP, BABY! YEAAAH!
SAME OLD JOKE! SAME OLD JOKE!
BEAT IT, KIDS.
HO HO HO! OH, FAIRY GOD-MOTHER!
YOU SHOULDN'T HAVE! REALLY!
TRA LA LA LA!
OOOH, THEY DID THE PUMPKIN MASH! OOOH, IT WAS A VEGGIE PATCH SMASH!
HUH?

OOOH! ♪
I KNOW! YOU'RE GOING TO MAKE ME A CARRIAGE! ♪ ♫
STIR! ♪STIR!
DON'T COOK IT!!
SHALL WE GO? ♪
YES! I'VE BEEN WAITING... ♫
AND-A-THREE!
GO!
DING-A DING-A RANG-A LANG-A
RAT TAT TAT
RANG-A LANG-A DING-A DONG
UH...
HEY, I'M HERE!
IT'S ARALE!

IT'S GATCHAN! ♪
PEE PEE POO-POO POO PEH POH! ♫
TIT TAT AND A RAT-TAT-TAT! ♫
♪ KIIIIN! KI KI KI, KIIIIN!
TUT TUT TUT
VABOOM
FSST FSST
MAY ALL YOUR BOMBS ♫ COME TRUUUUE!
BOOM
... ♫
HEY, YOU'RE AN IDIOT!
HEY, YOU'RE A PIG!
OOOH, THE SUN IS SHINING! ♫
GOOD ♫ WORK, GUYS!
EEEK! ♫
BOO! ♫
YOU KNOW HOW LONG I'VE WAITED!? ♪
HEEEY! THAT'S NOT HOW THE STORY GO-O-O-ES! ♫

OH, NO! WE'VE RUN OUT OF PAGES!
WHAAAT!?
WHOOOO ARE YOU?
YOU SCARED ME!
I'M THE REAL FAIRY GODMOTHER!
PLEASE, CONTROL YOURSELF! EVERYONE'S WATCHING!
YES!!
JUST ONE PANEL LEFT! GOOD LUCK!
WHEEEE!
MY!
OOOH!
COULD THIS REALLY BE ME!?
COCK-A-DOODLE-DOO!
FWOMP
SHUFFLE SHUFFLE
ALL DONE, ALL DONE.
YAWN. YAWN.
THE ENNNND!

Dr. Slump SUPER Quiz

♡Penguin Village Junior High School Entrance Exam

Part One

If any of the following statements is true, fill in the corresponding box under the O in the answers section below. If it's not true, fill in the box under the X.

1. Arale's energy source is Panvita-A.
2. Akane and Taro are in the same grade.
3. The Doctor built a time machine called the "Time Slipper."
4. King Nikochan often speaks with an Eastern European accent.
5. Suppaman and Parzan's relationship is one of mutual respect.
6. Gatchan's full name is Gamera Norimaki.
7. Dr. Mashirito's robot is Caramel Man 001.
8. Taro's dad used to be a cop.
9. The super dog from space was named "Poop."
10. Taro loves baseball.

Part Two

Read the following questions 1-5 very carefully. Choose your answers from A, B, or C and place a check in the appropriate box below.

1. What is Arale's secret weapon?
   A. The Uh-ho-hoy Cannon
   B. The N'cha Cannon
   C. The Bye'cha Cannon

2. What is Taro and Akane's relationship?
   A. Cousins
   B. Lovers
   C. Total strangers

3. What is Taro's mother's name?
   A. Daizu (soybean)
   B. Azuki (sweetbean)
   C. Mame (bean)

4. Where are King Nikochan's ears?
   A. Behind his legs
   B. On his palms
   C. In his mouth

5. Who was in the same preschool class as Superman?
   A. Bubibinman
   B. Suppaman
   C. Dr. Mashirito

Answers on page 194.

Answer Sheet: Use a No. 2 pencil!

[Part One] 5 Points

	○×	○×	○×	○×	○×
	1. □□	2. □□	3. □□	4. □□	5. □□
	6. □□	7. □□	8. □□	9. □□	10. □□

[Part Two] 10 Points

A B C	A B C	A B C	A B C	A B C
1. □□□	2. □□□	3. □□□	4. □□□	5. □□□

Nickname		Hobbies	[ ] Autograph collecting [ ] Napping [ ] Brawling [ ] Marathon phone calling	[ ] Bean sowing [ ] Nose picking [ ] Pimple popping [ ] Being bad [ ] Other	Points	

Spluk Spluk Phoo Phoo

ARALE
AKANE
ARALE

OCTO-BALLS
OCTO-BALLS
MAKUSA
ARALE
?
LE
NOD
?
BLOOP
SQUISH
SQUISH

WUUUG
SPOK
VWEEEEN
POOOT
VWEE VWEE
GULP
SNAP
FWUP FWUP
THUD THUD
...?
VWEEN
YAR!
USA
HEEEH ...
SPLUK SPLUK
KUS

READ THIS WAY
PAT PAT
?
?
ARALE
ARALE
AAAAGH!
BONK
THUD
THUD
SPLUK

PHOO
PHOO
SPLUK
ARALE
PHOO
PHOO
HIII...N
PHOO
PHOO
COFFEE
Pot

RIBBIT
ARALE
RIBBIT
RIBBIT
BOING
ARALE
ROLL ROLL...
ARALE
ARALE
SPLUK
P
...
PHOO
PHOO

SPLUK
SPLUK
VAZOOM
?!
?
ZAAAP!
?
?
?
SPLASH
?!

READ THIS WAY
WUMP WUMPA WUMP
WUMP WUMPA WUMP
WHOMP
GAR GAR
...

SPLUK
SPLUK
SPLUK!
ZZZ
ZZZ

READ THIS WAY

Dr. Slump SUPER Quiz

♡ Penguin Village High School Entrance Exam

Part One

Read the following statements carefully and determine the truthfulness of the underlined sections as best you can.

A. The exchange student from Metropolis Island was named Mr. Stop.
B. Senbei often eats ramen noodles.
C. The monster Dodongadon appeared in Penguin Village, which is when Koita Ojo of the Ulteeny Police Force came and transformed into Kintaman.
D. When Kinoko's father ate her jumbo Strawberry Shortcake, she turned bad, bought cigarettes, and got a light from Gamera, who was passing by.
E. The first restaurant Arale ever went to was the Coffee Pot. The first thing she ever broke was a telephone pole.

Part Two

Read the following questions (1-5) very carefully. Choose your answers from A, B, or C and place a check in the appropriate box below.

1. When is Arale's birthday?
   A. The 17th of Flying Fish
   B. The 9th of Seagull
   C. The 15th of Blue Whale

2. Where do the Norimakis live?
   A. No. 1, Armadillo Drive
   B. No. 1, Flying Chipmunk Drive
   C. No. 1, Flying Squirrel Drive

3. How many people are on the Penguin Village police force?
   A. Four
   B. Five
   C. Seven

4. Which school is located in Penguin Village?
   A. Junior High School
   B. Middle School
   C. Middle High School

5. Why doesn't Parzan wear clothes, even when he's cold?
   A. He likes the look.
   B. He doesn't want to be mistaken for Suppaman.
   C. To stay fit

Answers on page 194.

Answer Sheet: Use a No. 2 pencil!

[Part One] 5 Points

	○	×
1.	□	□
2.	□	□
3.	□	□
4.	□	□
5.	□	□
6.	□	□
7.	□	□
8.	□	□
9.	□	□
10.	□	□

[Part Two] 10 Points

	A	B	C
1.	□	□	□
2.	□	□	□
3.	□	□	□
4.	□	□	□
5.	□	□	□

Name		Talents	[ ] Specium Rays [ ] U-Die Bazooka [ ] Penguinery Art [ ] Toe curling [ ] Other	Talents	

Mammoth Midori
Part 1

DRIZZLE DRIZZLE
ONE FINE DAY...
ZIZIIP
FSST
PHOO

READ THIS WAY

BOING
WHA--!?
EH!?
VWEE
UNH...
KRASH
WAS THAT...
...MY BIG-SMALL RAY GUN?
FLIT FLIT
HEE HEE

READ THIS WAY

TEE HEE!
I KNEW IT.
CIGAR
YOU TRICKED ME, DARN IT!
ARALE!!! GRRAH!
...BEHAVE !?
KLIK
WHY CAN'T YOU...
LITTLE

READ THIS WAY

...WAS OUT FOR A WALK...
IT'S RAINING!
IT'S POURING!
SPLISH
SPLASH
THE OLD MAN IS... ♪
...WHEN SHE SUDDENLY FELL ON HER FACE!
SPLOOCK
...AND HAD TO BE TAKEN AWAY.
AM-BUU AM-BUU
LAAAANCE
YOU NEVER KNOW WHEN TO STOP, DO YOU?
DON'T YOU HAVE ANYTHING BETTER TO DO THAN BUG ME ALL DAY?
PEN GUIN

BREEEP BREEEP
HEY! PHONE!
HULLO?
THIS IS NORIMAKI...
IT'S ME...
...AKIRA TORIYAMA... AGE 27... LOOKING FOR A WIFE.
WHAT DO YOU WANT?
YOU KNOW THAT TEACHER YOU LIKE? MS. YAMABUKI?
SHE'S IN THE HOSPITAL.
WHOA!
HEY!
ARE YOU SURE!?
I'M THE AUTHOR. OF COURSE I'M SURE.
THINK I'M LYING? READ THE LAST PAGE AGAIN!

MIDORI...!!
PATAPATAAA...
GOAT HOSPITAL
WE'LL FIX ANYTHING!
RADIOS, CAMERAS, AUTOM
INJURIES, ETC...
GOAT HOSPI
MS. YAMA-BUKI!!!
N'CHA!!!
AH!

READ THIS WAY

Buzz buzz.
I BELIEVE IT ENTERED THROUGH THE MOUTH WHILE THE PATIENT SLEPT.
MIDORI YAMABUKI
THE SQUEETO, OR MOSQUITO, IS HERE.
La dee da.
♪La dee.
ONCE INSIDE, THE SQUEETO TOOK ADVANTAGE OF THIS PESTICIDE-FREE ENVIRONMENT AND SET UP SHOP. IT WAS AN EASY LIFE, WITH ALL THE BLOOD HE COULD DRINK!
...
THEY ALL BEGAN DRINKING AT ONCE, ROBBING THE PATIENT OF HER BLOOD!
SLUMP
EVENTUALLY, THE SQUEETO LAID EGGS THAT HATCHED INTO LARVAE, WHICH GREW INTO OTHER SQUEETOS.
QUICK! THE ANES-THESIA!
I DON'T WANT TO DIE FROM THAT!
YEEARGH! THAT'S GROSS!

AS I WAS SAYING...
...WE CAN'T OPERATE. THE SQUEETOS WOULD ESCAPE TO ANOTHER PART OF THE BODY.
SLUMP
PEN GUIN
BONK
WELL, OF COURSE...
BUT WE'RE A LITTLE LARGE FOR THAT!
Dummy...
CAN'T YOU GO INSIDE THE BODY AND SPRAY 'EM OUT?
NO, WE'RE NOT!
I MEAN, WE ARE! BUT NOT FOR LONG!
ARALE
TO BE CONTINUED...

Dr. Slump SUPER Quiz

♡ Penguin University Entrance Exam

Part One

Answer the following questions:

1. What was the pen name of the unlucky older guy who kidnapped Arale?
2. Name the unlucky assassin who attempted to do in Arale.
3. Which school did the unlucky gang boss--the one who went on a date with Arale--go to?
4. How many students attend Penguin Village Junior High?
5. Name Peasuke's first love.
6. What was Akane eating when she first met Arale?
7. Name the reporter at PCB Television.
8. Name the zoo in Penguin Village.
9. Name the apartment complex where Ms. Yamabuki lives.
10. Name the unlucky vampire who sneaked into the Norimaki household.

Part Two

Read the following questions (1-5) very carefully. Choose your answers from A, B, or C and place a check in the appropriate box below.

1. What is the name of the fearsome lady cop at the Penguin Village Police Station?
   A. Polly Buckets
   B. Pony Tail
   C. Polly Propane

2. Where does Dr. Mashirito's mother live?
   A. Saitama Prefecture
   B. Chiba Prefecture
   C. Ibaraki Prefecture

3. What is Kintaman's secret attack?
   A. Special Head Slam
   B. Special Leg Crush
   C. Special Finger-Cross Punch

4. What panties has Ms. Yamabuki not worn?
   A. Strawberry Panties
   B. Hippo Panties
   C. Bear Panties

5. What did Arale think the first bear she ever saw was?
   A. A caterpillar
   B. A spider
   C. An earthworm

Answers on page 194.

Answer Sheet: Use a No. 2 pencil!

[Part One] 5 Points

1. 2. 3. 4. 5.
6. 7. 8. 9. 10.

[Part Two] 10 Points

1. A B C ☐☐☐ 2. A B C ☐☐☐ 3. A B C ☐☐☐ 4. A B C ☐☐☐ 5. A B C ☐☐☐

Name		Checkup	Height in. Weight lbs. Butt elevation in. Smarts [ ] Yup [ ] Sure [ ] Huh Eyes [ ] Good [ ] Bad [ ] Like Toriyama's	Points	

Mammoth Midori: Part 2

Mammoth Midori Part 2

Ho-yo! What big thighs!
Koo pee pah pee pee!

ALL RIGHT! READY?
HERE GOES!
BIIIG
VWOOM
HO-YO!?
I TOLD YOU TO HIT THE SMALL SWITCH!
I JUST WANTED TO SEE THINGS GET BIG.

READ THIS WAY

LET'S TRY WAVING THIS DELICIOUS GOAT'S BUTTER!
GAAH
IT OPENED!
WOW, SHE MUST BE HUNGRY.
KIIN
COME BACK SOON, Y'HEAR?
ARALE
WHAT'S THIS, DOCTOR?
A THROAT WIENER.
WHAT'S THIS?
CURRY
SPAGHETTI
FISH
STEAK
SOUP
CUTLETS
ESCARGOT
MENU
MENU
THE CAFETERIA.

READ THIS WAY
LET'S PLAY HIDE-AND-SEEK!
WE'RE IN THE STOMACH!
AH, IT'S GETTING WIDER.
WHY WASN'T I INVITED?
SO HEARTLESS...
A-HA!
SHE ATE BEEF STEW LAST NIGHT.
OY!
HUH?
OKAY! I'M HIDING! FIND ME!
STOP PLAYING AROUND!

ACK!
KNOCK WHEN YOU ENTER SOMEBODY'S HOUSE!
WHADDAYA THINK YOU'RE DOING!?
WHO'RE YOU CALLING "PIN-WORM"!?
SO WHAT ARE YOU? PINWORMS?
TOO LATE! GAH!
HELLO-O-O! ANYBODY HOME?
LEAVE MY MIDORI! NOW!
THAT'S IT, SQUEETO! YOU PICKED THE WRONG BLOOD TO SUCK!
YEEEARGH!
PHOOT PHOOT
THIS BUG SPRAY'S FOR YOU!

READ THIS WAY
OOOH!
KOFF
BZZZ
KOFF
OKAY! ALL CLEAR!
WE DID IT! WE DID IT!
BANZAI! BANZAI!
AND YOU DID IT BY YOURSELF FOR ONCE, DOCTOR!
ARALE
PENGUIN
ALL RIGHT!
LET'S GO HOME!
YAY!
PENGUIN VILLAGERS!
TODAY'S RECYCLING DAY!
BRING OUT YOUR SCRAP PAPER!

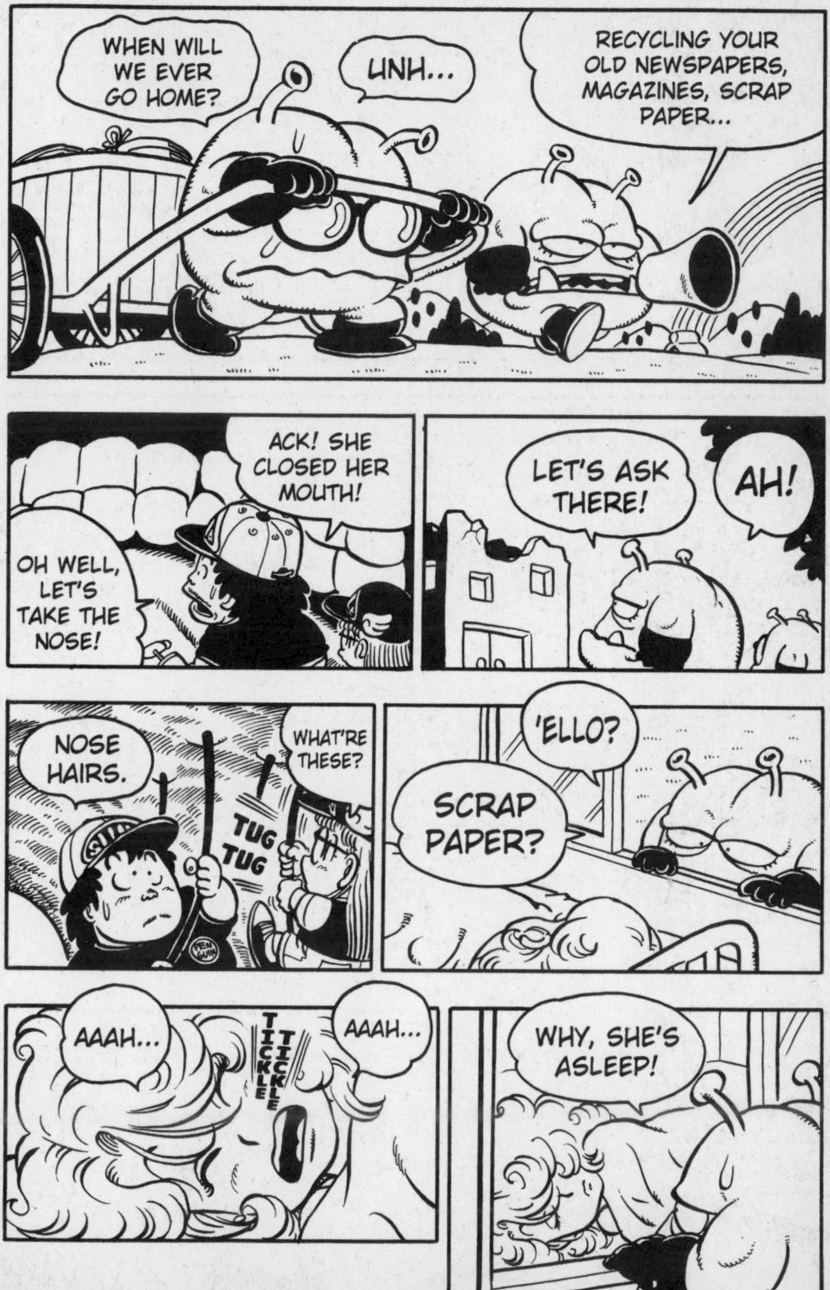
RECYCLING YOUR OLD NEWSPAPERS, MAGAZINES, SCRAP PAPER...
UNH...
WHEN WILL WE EVER GO HOME?
AH!
LET'S ASK THERE!
ACK! SHE CLOSED HER MOUTH!
OH WELL, LET'S TAKE THE NOSE!
'ELLO?
SCRAP PAPER?
WHAT'RE THESE?
NOSE HAIRS.
TUG TUG
WHY, SHE'S ASLEEP!
AAAH...
TICKLE TICKLE
AAAH...

READ THIS WAY

WHAA-CHOO!!
WHOA!
WHEE
FILTHY GIRL!
SCARED ME TO DEATH...
WHA...
WHAT JUST HAPPENED?
HO-YO...
HEY, DID YOU SAY SOMETHING?
NUTTIN' SIR.
WHAT THE HECK KIND OF ORGAN IS THIS!?

WE GOTTA FIND THE WAY OUT, QUICK!
KIIIN
MY STOMACH HURTS...
...
YOO HOO! COME ON OUT!
THE HOUR'S ALMOST UP!
ICK! THIS PLACE STINKS!
OOOH...
I... I GOTTA POOP!
HUH?

I COULDN'T HOLD IT IN, OKAY?
QUIET, YOU.
OH, WOE IS I!
YOU MAY BE KING, BUT YOU GO TOO FAR!
IT'S BARBARIC! POOPING IN THE WILD!
HOW SHAME-FUL!
HA-HA-HAIR DOO-DOO-DOO...
GET OVER IT ALREADY!
I'M SO EMBAR-RASSED...
SPLOOSH
I WONDER WHAT IT IS?
ONE HOUR!

Dr. Slump SUPER Quiz

♡Penguin Imperial Co., Ltd. Employment Entrance Exam

Part One

Answer the following questions as best you can.

1. Name Arale's classmate, the one who always wears a mask.
2. Name the chief of the Penguin Village Police Station.
3. Name the thunder deity who does the morning weather for Penguin Village TV.
4. Why did Senbei hide the Future Camera?
5. How many Wonderbuses pass through Penguin Village every day?
6. Name Bubibinman's home planet.
7. Name King Nikochan home planet.
8. Name the volcano to the west of Penguin Village.
9. Which television station on Metropolis Island was Senbei suppose to appear on?
10. Name the hospital that healed space-dog Poop.
11. Name Akane's father.
12. What did King Nikochan mistake for a space ship in the Norimakis' house?
13. Name the pig who sometimes appears wearing sunglasses.
14. Name an animal Senbei doesn't like.
15. Name something Gatchan can't eat.
16. What is Taro's future occupation, according to the Future Camera?
17. What's Akane's favorite drink?
18. The milk deliveries in Penguin Village are Mosquito Milk and _____ Milk.
19. What was Suppaman's nickname in elementary school?
20. Name the love potion that Senbei's father taught him to make via a videotape he left before he died?

Answers on page 194.

Write 'em all!!!	Part One 5 Points				
		1.	2.	3.	4.	5.
		6.	7.	8.	9.	10.
		11.	12.	13.	14.	15.
		16.	17.	18.	19.	20.

Name		Education	[ ] Preschool [ ] Elementary School [ ] Junior High [ ] High School	[ ] College [ ] Dropout [ ] Top in the Class [ ] Dumb for Life	Points	

Am I

Wicked Strong!?

THERE WAS ONCE A YOUTH WHO TRAVELED FROM VILLAGE TO VILLAGE, THROUGH AUTUMN WINDS, SEEKING OUT THE STRONG...
I'M THE AUTUMN WIND!
WOO! WOO!
WEEE OOOO
WOOO OOOO OOOOH
I TRAVEL FROM VILLAGE TO VILLAGE, BUT NONE CAN BEST ME.
HAVE I BECOME THE WORLD'S CHAMPION FIGHTER AT SUCH A YOUNG AGE?
BUT WHY DO I FEEL SO COLD?
IT'S AS IF THE AUTUMN WIND BLOWS RIGHT THROUGH MY SOUL.
SHIVER SHIVER
WHAT A WUSS!
MAYBE HE'S GOT A HOLE IN HIM.

READ THIS WAY

PERHAPS YOU NEED A DEMON-STRATION.
OH YEAH? THEM'S FIGHTING WORDS...
WOO
WHAT'S HE UP TO?
?
KRAK
EEP!!
COME AND GET IT!

READ THIS WAY

KLOP
OH MY!
HE'S SO GROOVY!
...
SSSHHH
HYAH!
...?

READ THIS WAY
ZING
FWIP
SNIK
I GET IT! YOU CUT THE LEAF!

HEY!!
BUT IT ISN'T CUT!!
...
...
ZING

READ THIS WAY

YAR!
BUN!
EEP!
ACK!
WATCH OUT!

READ THIS WAY

HEH...
ZING
AH!
SSS NUK
WOO! COOL!
CLAP CLAP CLAP
WHOA! THAT WAS CLOSE!
YAR!
!!
GRAH!!
YOW!!!
OOOH ...
OOOOOH ...

READ THIS WAY

END OF VOLUME 7

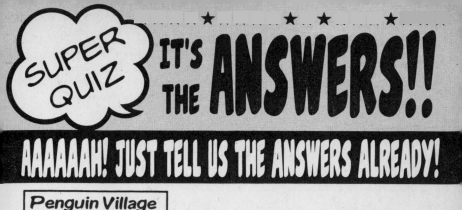

SUPER QUIZ IT'S THE ANSWERS!!

AAAAAAH! JUST TELL US THE ANSWERS ALREADY!

Penguin Village Day Care

[Answers]

Part One

1 ✕ 2 ✕ 3 ✕
4 ○ 5 ○ 6 ✕
7 ○ 8 ✕ 9 ○
10 ✕

Part Two

1 C 2 B 3 C
4 A 5 B

☆ Okay, at least you got 80 points... WHAT!? 30!?

Wh-What the...!? I know! You've been reading comics in the bookstore again, haven't you!? Get up there and erase that chalkboard... with your face!

Penguin Village Elementary

[Answers]

Part One

1 ○ 2 ○ 3 ○
4 ✕ 5 ○ 6 ○
7 ✕ 8 ○ 9 ○
10 ○

Part Two

1 A 2 B 3 C
4 B 5 C

☆ This is elementary school we're talking about, so you'd better get 70 points. Ever had to write on a chalkboard...with your face!? It's not pleasant, let me tell you.

Penguin Junior High

[Answers]

Part One

1 ✕ 2 ✕ 3 ○
4 ✕ 5 ✕ 6 ✕
7 ○ 8 ○ 9 ○
10 ○

Part Two

1 B 2 A 3 C
4 A 5 A

☆ Sick of all these easy questions yet!? Wha--!? You still got less than 70!? Prepare to have your gym shorts pulled down to the knees, losers!

Dr. SLUMP™

♥ WHICH OF YOU DROPOUTS WILL WIN!?

Penguin High School

(Answers)

Part One

1× 2○ 3○
4× 5× 6×
7× 8○ 9○
10×

Part Two

1A 2C 3B
4B 5B

☆ So things are a little harder, eh? This is **high** school, man. It's supposed to be hard! Addition? We've got multiplication! Get 60 points at least and I'll be happy.

Penguin University

(Answers)

Part One

1. Dr. Monster 2. The Shiverman
3. Kanariya High 4. 65
5. Hiyoko 6. Bubble gum
7. Kura'aku Kenta 8. WILD LAND
9. Angulrus Apartments 10. Trampire

Part Two

1A 2B 3A
4C 5A

☆ Hah! Weren't expecting things to get tough so quick, eh? University's no joke, folks. Sixty points is a pretty decent achievement.
Get 100 points, and you can give your classmates all the wedgies you want!

Penguin Imperial Co., Ltd.

(Answers)

Part One

1. Nejishiki 2. Captain Gyaos
3. Thunder Ogre Goronbo
4. Because he goes bald in the future.
5. Five 6. Okaka-umeboshi 7. Planet Nikochan
8. Mt. Flapflap 9. KLOD 4
10. Goat Hospital 11. Kon Kimidori
12. The toilet 13. Oinkety Oink
14. Dogs 15. Rubber
16. Police officer 17. Super Punch
18. Fly 19. Suppa-Mouth
20. Fall-Down-Go-Boom Love Potion

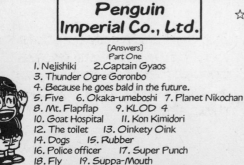

☆ Didn't get any, did ya!? Yeah, they were pretty obscure questions.
Get 50 points and you're in the company. Get 100 points and you're out, because anyone who got all these answers obviously spent way too much time reading manga instead of studying!

Later!

In The Next Volume

Senbei builds a miniature house that influences events in his real house. The madness begins when Gatchan pokes a finger through the miniature roof, and a giant finger suddenly comes crashing through the ceiling above Senbei! All this and more in the next fun-filled volume of **Dr. Slump**!

Available in July 2006!